Why this book?

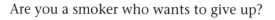

Are you a smoker who wants to give up?

Are you concerned about the health implications of smoking, but not ready to stop yet?

If so, this book will give you all you need to know – including:

- what cigarettes actually contain and why they are harmful

- what the short-term and longer-term damage can be

- all the different forms of help that are available

- how to set realistic goals and achieve them

- how to avoid relapsing

- how to beat smoking once and for all.

Full of tried and tested advice, it will enable you to take the first steps out of being a smoker – and towards a healthier, happier, and richer you.

First Steps out of **Smoking**

Dr Simon Atkins

LION

All advice given is for information only and should not be treated as a substitute for personal medical advice.

Published by Lion Books
an imprint of
Lion Hudson plc
Wilkinson House, Jordan Hill Road,
Oxford OX2 8DR, England
www.lionhudson.com/lion

ISBN 978 0 7459 5621 3
e-ISBN 978 0 7459 5785 2

First edition 2013

Acknowledgments
Diagrams pp. 51, 99 © Sam Atkins

A catalogue record for this book is available from the British Library

Printed and bound in Malta, October 2013, LH28

Dedicated to the memory
of my dad and grandpa,
both unashamed quitters.

Contents

Introduction

If there's one thing you can't accuse smoking of – and, believe me, I will spend the next ninety or so pages mentioning a multitude of things that you can accuse it of – it's of being un-cool.

Whether it's Rolling Stone Ronnie Wood prowling around a concert stage strumming "Brown Sugar" with one hand while holding a cigarette in the other, Ernest Hemingway tapping a masterpiece into his typewriter with a half-smoked, glowing stub in the corner of his mouth, or Bette Davis smouldering in a black-and-white movie, still with a wisp of smoke curling in front of her legendary eyes, their filter-tipped accessories unquestionably add a touch of glamour and street cred. Smoking, like the Stones themselves, is rock and roll.

And tobacco advertising often used to focus on this cool image, most notably with the Marlboro Man, the rugged cowboy pictured drawing on a cigarette as he worked his horses in the great outdoors. It was an image that helped turn Marlboro into the world's leading brand.

In my line of work as a doctor, however, the images I see of smokers are far from cool. I regularly see people whose years of inhaling have helped fur up their arteries, leading to paralysing strokes or crushing heart attacks. These once-fit individuals now need someone else to feed them and wipe their backsides. There are those whose smoke-ravaged lungs no longer take in enough air with each breath, who puff and pant with the smallest exertion, and need an oxygen cylinder close by just to climb the stairs. Riding a horse in the great outdoors would kill them.

Then there are the countless people whose love of cigarettes has led to mutations in the cells of any number of parts of their body, turning them cancerous. Be it cancer of the mouth, throat, lungs, bladder, or guts, the effect is the same: a long, slow death as the relentlessly dividing cancer cells steal the energy from their bodies and strip flesh from their bones.

This was what eventually happened to the actor who played the famous Marlboro Man: he died of lung cancer in 1992. And it happens to millions of others around the world every year. People's lives cut short simply because of a habit they couldn't – or wouldn't – quit.

Smoking may look cool in the movies, but when you end your days breathing through a hole in your throat because a surgeon has had to cut out your cancerous larynx, that coolness has long gone.

Of course, if you are a smoker, you will know all of this already. In fact, unless you've just teleported in from Mars in a UFO on a mission to observe our strange little species, you will have been repeatedly made aware by doctors, nurses, the government, and the media about how bad your habit is for you. But, for some reason, this may not be enough to make you want to kick the habit.

Perhaps you are young, you keep fit, eat your greens, and go to bed early with a cup of hot cocoa every night, and believe that all these healthy pursuits will militate against your one, tiny unhealthy activity. We all feel invincible when we are young. There will be plenty of time in the future to pack it in, so why worry now?

You might believe your stressful lifestyle means that you couldn't cope without your trusty cigarettes to help you wind down at the end of the day or relax in a crisis. At least they keep you going and you haven't had to hit the bottle!

Or it may be that you just enjoy smoking too much. You have friends who smoke and there's nothing nicer than kicking back with your mates over a glass of wine or a freshly brewed coffee and savouring a cigarette while you do so.

You may have other reasons, unique to you, for carrying on. Until those reasons seem less important than your health and your lifespan, then you won't consider quitting. And that is your choice. No matter how much browbeating you get from others, you won't want – or be able – to stop. So, if that's you, maybe see what else I have to say on the subject in the other chapters for now and then tuck this book away on your shelves until you feel the time is right and it might come in handy.

If, however, you are ready to quit and your reasons *for* smoking are finally outweighed by those *against*, then this is the book for you. Right now!

Some of you may not want any help at all. You've made your mind up and you're just going to stop – go "cold turkey" as it's called – and that's all there is to it. Many people find that works for them. My dad, for example, decided to stop smoking when I was born and didn't ever light up another cigarette from that day on, despite a previous forty-per-day habit and the lack of nicotine replacement therapies to help beat cravings in 1967. For others, though, willpower alone is only part of the process and some sort of medical help to counteract the withdrawal symptoms will be vital.

In the following chapters we will look at the different types of help that are available, including nicotine replacement therapies (NRT), pills, e-cigarettes, and smartphone apps. We'll also look at the psychological support that's available and cover alternative remedies and whether they have anything genuine to offer when it comes to quitting cigarettes. What really works and what doesn't? There is no point you wasting your time, trying a treatment that is doomed to fail.

But, first, let's consider some hard facts about the full extent of the danger that cigarettes pose to health, followed by a look at why smoking is such a hard habit to break.

 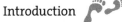

1

Why smoking is so bad for you

As I write, another food scandal is hitting the news headlines and causing widespread alarm and outrage: they've found traces of horse meat in our beefburgers!

It's turned up in frozen ready meals from supermarkets and on the lunch plates of school children and frail hospital patients. Not only that, but these products have been manufactured by some of Britain's most established and respected brands. In fact, there is an extremely high chance, we are being told, that anyone who's recently devoured any pre-prepared meal alleged to contain succulent pieces of prime beef is more likely to have enjoyed mouthfuls of meat from an animal that used to go "neigh" rather than "moo"!

The amount of media coverage this has generated has been massive, even though no one has or will come to any harm from this mislabelling of our cherished convenience foods.

Imagine, then, the furore that would be generated if a manufacturer put products on the shelves in our high streets that they actually knew would not only cause harm but lead directly to the deaths of almost half of the people who regularly consumed them. Products that contained chemicals so toxic that they caused lethal mutations in human body cells, destruction of blood vessel walls, and irreversible damage to the air spaces in lungs. Products known to kill, maim, and disable because they are proven to cause heart attacks, strokes, and cancer.

Just imagine the public outcry, the newspaper column inches that would be published, the TV documentaries bringing the full extent of the scandal to light. The manufacturers would surely be put out of business and their CEOs given hefty prison sentences.

Imagine again. Because that is exactly what cigarette manufacturers do every single day and the only hefty thing they get is profit. And if you want to see for yourself what they put into cigarettes, then all the details are in Appendix A.

Smoking and cancer

Until the 1950s smoking was thought to be a harmless pastime. Watch any old black-and-white movie and you'll see most of the cast blissfully puffing away on one cigarette after the other, mirroring society's habits as a whole at that time. But all that changed after a famous British study by Richard Doll and Austin Bradford Hill, looking at the causes of death of 40,000 of the country's smokers, all of whom were doctors.

After analysing years of data, they concluded in 1956 that the death rate from lung cancer among heavy smokers was an enormous twenty times greater than it was for non-smokers. And when Doll and other colleagues at the Medical Research Council reported results of nearly half a century's further research in 2004, they came to some very startling conclusions:

- Smoking lowered life expectancy by an average of ten years.

- Around half of those who smoked were killed by their habit.

And that wasn't all. They also found that the following fatal illnesses were related to smoking:

- lung cancer

- chronic obstructive airways disease (chronic bronchitis and emphysema)

- coronary heart disease (angina and heart attacks)

- strokes

- cancers of the mouth, bladder, liver, pancreas, kidney, stomach, and cervix.

(Source: Medical Research Council, 2007)

Other health implications

Since Doll and Hill highlighted the health risks of smoking, more medical problems have come to light that are a direct effect of people taking up the habit.

Here's a quick run through of some of the bits of your body it can non-fatally but often permanently damage.

Eyes

Smokers are more prone to cataracts and macular degeneration, which can reduce eyesight and potentially lead to blindness. (The macula is the part of the retina at the back of your eyes that is responsible for seeing fine detail.)

Mouth

Smoking gives you bad breath and painful mouth ulcers, stains your teeth and tongue, and makes you more prone to gum disease (which can cause you to lose teeth).

Skin

Cigarettes reduce blood supply to the skin, making it paler and much more wrinkled than the skin of non-smokers.

Circulation
Smoking puts up blood pressure, which in turn adds to the risk of heart attacks and strokes.

Genitals
Couples who smoke are far more likely to have fertility problems than those who don't. And here's the biggie (or not in this case!): men who smoke are 50 per cent more likely to be impotent than non-smokers.

In short, if the idea of getting cancer doesn't put you off smoking, then surely the risk of being a toothless, wrinkled individual with bad breath and sexual dysfunction must make you want to think twice about lighting up!

Financial implications
Financially, too, smoking is a killer. According to a British Heart Foundation study in 2009, all of the smoking-related illnesses mentioned above cost the National Health Service an estimated £5 billion per year – 5.5 per cent of its total budget.

Just think how much crippling disability could be prevented if some of that £5 billion could be spent on hip replacements for the elderly instead of on smokers' self-inflicted diseases. Or how many infertile couples could be given the life-changing chance of having a baby. Not to mention the thousands who would benefit if that money could be spent on such worthy causes as cataract surgery, better mental health services, or children's cancer treatments.

On a more personal note, just think of the impact your habit has on your individual finances. At present prices, a ten-a-day habit sets you back in the region of £1,340 over twelve months. That's costing you what could be a lovely family holiday every year, or the chance to put something towards that top-of-the-range car you always promised yourself. (Source: NHS Choices Smoking Cost Calculator)

Passive smoking

Smoking is not just bad for you and your wallet; it's also known to be bad for all those around you. Research into passive smoking has produced evidence that an alarming number of health problems occur as a direct result of other people breathing in the smoke that you have just breathed out.

Unborn children

Passive smoking by pregnant women can cause reduced growth and affect organ development in their babies.

Babies and children

Passive smoking is known to be a risk factor for cot death in babies (sudden infant death syndrome) and can cause ear and chest infections, and worsen asthma in all children.

Adults

Passive smoking by adults puts them at a higher risk of all of the illnesses that affect smokers themselves, from lung and heart disease through to all the cancers mentioned above.

Smoking is bad, full stop

I hope that this chapter has illustrated how the dangers of smoking are very real and need to be taken seriously. Although your Uncle Bert may have smoked eighty a day until his hundredth birthday without having so much as a tickle in his throat to show for it, that does not disprove what I have just said. All it proves is that Uncle Bert was a very lucky man. You, on the other hand, may not be so lucky: the odds are very much against you on this one!

Mythbuster

Other forms of smoking are not as bad for you as cigarettes.

Roll-your-own cigarettes (roll-ups)

People often think that these cigarettes are less harmful because there is less tobacco in each roll-up than in a factory-made cigarette. However, when researchers have compared the two types, the quantity of toxins inhaled appears to be the same because roll-up smokers tend to take more frequent and deeper puffs on each cigarette and often do not use filters.

Cigars

Another common misconception is that cigars are safer than cigarettes because smoking them doesn't usually involve inhaling smoke deep into the lungs. However, both nicotine and toxins are still absorbed into your bloodstream through the tissues of the mouth, and so nicotine addiction, heart and lung disease, and cancers are just as common in cigar smokers as in people who just smoke cigarettes. And some pretty nasty mouth cancers are actually more common.

Pipes

You've guessed it! Smoking a pipe is no better for you either and puts you at risk of all the side effects of cigarettes too.

Cannabis

And the final myth to bust is that smoking a joint is not as bad for your health as smoking a cigarette.

It's actually worse for you.

In 2012 the British Lung Foundation found that the puff of an average cannabis smoker was two-thirds larger and held for four times longer than the puff of a cigarette smoker, and, as a result, smoking one cannabis cigarette carries the same risk of developing lung cancer as smoking twenty ordinary tobacco cigarettes.

2

Why do people smoke?

If we all know it's so bad for us, why on earth do so many people continue to enjoy puffing away on their cigarettes? And why are we still seeing so many new recruits taking up the habit?

Smoking statistics

There are lots of smokers out there. It's estimated that there are over a billion smokers around the world who between them have inhaled 43 trillion cigarettes over the past ten years.

In the United Kingdom the numbers stack up as follows:

• Some 21 per cent of adult men and 19 per cent of adult women are smokers.

- Smoking prevalence is highest among 20–24 year-olds.

- Smoking rates are markedly higher among poorer people: 13 per cent of adults in managerial and professional occupations smoke, compared with 28 per cent in manual occupations.

(Source: ASH website)

Rates in the USA are very similar, with 45 million adults (19 per cent of the adult population) being smokers. The age and gender proportions are roughly the same and it is again more common in those with manual occupations or who are out of work. (Source: CDC website)

Across the border in Canada, the figures are slightly lower. They show that currently around 17 per cent of the total population are smokers, with 19.7 per cent of men and 15 per cent of women indulging in the habit. (Source: Health Canada website)

And if we head Down Under, we find that 16.4 per cent of Australian men and 13.9 per cent of Australian women over the age of fourteen are smokers. In New Zealand, the figures are higher at 20.3 per cent and 16.2 per cent for non-Maori men and women respectively, and 39.3 per cent and 48.3 per cent for Maori men and women. (Sources: cancercouncil.com.au and health.govt.nz)

When these smoking figures are translated into hard cash, the sums of money in question are astounding. In 2010, the combined profit for the six leading tobacco companies was US$35.1 billion. This equalled the profits of Coca-Cola, Microsoft, and McDonald's added together in the same year and is about the same as the gross domestic product (GDP) of whole countries such as Poland, Saudi Arabia, and Sweden. (Source: World Lung Foundation Website)

Why do most people start smoking?

In early 2013 a group of Italian researchers published the results of surveys they had been carrying out every year from 2005 to 2010 on thousands of people over the age of fifteen, to analyse the reasons they had for taking up smoking. They found that the overwhelming majority (just over 60 per cent) of those they interviewed had started simply because of the influence of their friends.

One-third of smokers had started before the age of sixteen, with a massive two-thirds picking up the habit by the time they hit eighteen.

Other reasons given were:

- For enjoyment and satisfaction – 15.6 per cent.

- To feel mature and independent – 9.0 per cent.

- Because of the influence of partner/family – 6.6 per cent.

- Because of stress – 2.5 per cent.

- To feel more secure – 1.9 per cent.

- For curiosity – 1.8 per cent.

(Source: R. Muttarak and colleagues, *European Journal of Cancer Prevention*, 2013)

Similar reasons have been given by smokers all over the world. The idea that smoking makes you look cool, mature, and independent is a particular favourite of teenage smokers, and many young women believe it helps them stay slim.

Why is smoking enjoyable?

The key ingredient in cigarettes that makes smoking such a pleasant experience is nicotine. This chemical is found in the roots of the tobacco plant, where it acts as a natural insecticide. It is named after a French ambassador to Portugal, Jean Nicot de Villemain, who first introduced his countrymen to tobacco that he'd been given by a Brazilian in the 1500s.

When you draw on a cigarette, the nicotine travels in the smoke particles directly into your lungs, from where it is rapidly absorbed into your bloodstream. It's then pumped through your arteries to your brain, where it attaches to receptors on nerve cells, triggering the release of a number of different chemicals called neurotransmitters.

It's one of these transmitters, called dopamine, that is responsible for producing the pleasurable feelings which follow seconds after you've inhaled and which, drag after drag, cause a reduction in levels of stress and anxiety. Dopamine is also responsible for similar feelings experienced by people who take amphetamines and cocaine, and is a powerful part of the addiction process.

How does addiction develop?

The brain quickly gets used to the nicotine and so more is needed, more frequently, in order to get the same "buzz" that lifts your mood and makes you feel relaxed. If there's a long gap between cigarettes (and this need only be around an hour), or if you try to cut down or stop, then the dopamine level in the brain soon drops, making you feel anxious, miserable, irritable, and lacking in concentration. A quick smoke will chase those feelings away, but each time you give in to this craving for relief, the addiction begins to take hold.

Brain changes are not the only triggers for nicotine addiction. The behaviours you associate with cigarettes also play a massive part in smoking becoming an addictive habit. For example, you may have a cigarette every time you brew yourself a coffee, get into the car, or have a beer with friends, or to kick-start the working day. These repetitive behaviours make you think you can't carry out these activities without a cigarette for company, and soon you develop a craving for a smoke every time you perform them. So, a cup of coffee or a drop of your favourite tipple will always taste better while smoking. The rush-hour drive becomes unthinkably stressful without a cigarette, and no restaurant meal will be complete without nipping outside for a drag or two.

Eventually, these associations become so entwined that they're like dance partners who can't possibly perform alone. And, without thinking, you light up a cigarette, right on cue, every time.

It then follows that in order to avoid, at first, disappointment and then, as the habit develops, full-on stress at having no cigarettes to hand in the car or by your bed, or wherever it is you crave one, you'll ensure you always have a pack to hand. And, as a result, the number of cigarettes inhaled each day will rise and the associations become virtually hard-wired into your brain's circuits.

And you're hooked!

And it's so easily done. I know, because in the past I used to have the odd puff with friends, usually when enjoying a beer. And although I was never a fully paid-up, regular smoker, the willpower needed to refuse the offer of a cigarette when friends light up has given me a valuable insight into how hard it must be for far more hardcore smokers to be successful in giving up.

Mythbuster

I can't give up smoking – it's far too hard to stop.
Most people find quitting is too hard when they rely on willpower alone, but you have a great chance of succeeding if you seek specialist help and use some of the great variety of stop-smoking treatments that are available.

3

The stages of successful quitting

Having covered the facts and figures about the dangers of smoking and the difficulties there can be in breaking your addiction to it, it's time to give some positive advice and show you how you can go about leaving the habit behind.

Unfortunately, the transformation you undergo from being a smoker to a non-smoker is not achieved in one miraculously easy step. It's not a smooth nought-to-sixty-in-thirty-seconds experience, where you rapidly leave your old habit way behind you like a tiny dot on the horizon. Rather it's a slow acceleration through all the gears with a few episodes of stalling at junctions and the odd emergency stop along the way. It can be a bumpy road, with most quitters behaving more like old bangers than supercars, chucking out unwanted clouds of smoke as they stutter towards their final destination.

To put this into more technical parlance, scientists studying the process you will go through have developed what's called the Transtheoretical Model of Quitting. And although that may sound a bit of a highfalutin way of describing things, I'm sure that as we look at what it means in plain English below, you will recognize yourself as being in one of the stages they've come up with.

Stage 1: Pre-contemplation

- You have no intention of quitting in the next six months.

- You are a happy smoker: any risks are far outweighed by the pleasure.

- If you did want to quit, you don't think you would have the willpower.

- You are scared of the potential side effects of giving up, such as weight gain.

- You are as likely to give up as pop to the moon.

Stage 2: Contemplation

- You've given it some thought.

- You're seriously tempted to give quitting a shot in the

next six months, although you have no plans as to how or exactly when this might happen.

- You are more concerned about the potential problems of smoking than you were.

- You care about how it might directly affect you in the future.

- You have researched ways to stop.

- You have talked to others who have given up successfully.

- You may have made a pact with a fellow smoker that you will try to quit together.

Stage 3: Preparation
D-Day is now actually approaching.

- You are planning to stop in the next month or so.

- You have taken some definite steps towards stopping.

- You have a clearer idea of what and who might help.

- You have researched further information.

- You may have visited your local health centre and talked to your family doctor or a practice nurse.

- You may even have signed up to a stop-smoking clinic.

- You may have set a quit date.

Stage 4: Action

- You have done it!

- For the next six months, you will be actively engaged in quitting.

- You are breaking the links between smoking and other activities.

- You are using all your quitting therapies.

You may well be fortunate enough to get through this stage in a few weeks, but don't be surprised if the process does take the best part of six months.

Stage 5: Maintenance

- You haven't had a cigarette for six months.

- You can handle all the cravings.

- You may be at risk of thinking that the odd puff won't do you any harm. It will – so don't!

- You need to keep your eyes fixed on your goal and continue to use all the measures that have helped you get this far.

Stage 6: Termination

Ta-dah! You're a non-smoker, you've beaten your cravings, and smoking is no longer a part of your life. But, again, you need to be aware of the risk of complacency here. One cheeky puff and you could be right back where you started, which, though not a disaster, would be a real disappointment after all the hard work you've put in.

If you follow these stages smoothly, then you are very lucky and definitely in the nought-to-sixty category. But you will be very unusual in doing this. For most people, the process will break down a number of times along the way. A crafty social smoke or a stressful day at work or home and your progress will stall. And you'll drop back to stage 2 again.

Don't let that put you off! As you'll see in the next few chapters, there is plenty of help out there to support you on this journey. So, if you've hit stage 3 and are prepared to give it a go, there's no time like the present to have a crack at it. Even if you're only at stage 2, it's not too early to check out the whys and wherefores of the quitting process, so that when you are ready for the off it will go a lot more smoothly.

Mythbuster

Cutting back on the number of cigarettes I smoke is good enough.
Unfortunately, it's not. Not only are you still taking in some of the toxins in cigarettes, but the evidence shows that you will probably tend to take more puffs and inhale more deeply each time you smoke in order to

get the same nicotine hit you had from smoking more cigarettes. So, in effect, you will be no better off at all.

What's next?
In the next section of the book we'll look at all the available treatments, giving an indication of what's been proven to work and how to access it.

First come the nicotine replacement therapies.

4

Nicotine replacement therapies (NRT)

This is the mainstay of support for people trying to stop smoking and certainly the most widely used method. It is available from pharmacies, online, and often on prescription, around the world.

How does it work?

It does exactly what it suggests by giving smokers who want to kick the habit a way of getting a dose of nicotine inside them without resorting to lighting up a cigarette. This nicotine then enters the bloodstream, heads to the brain, and attaches to the nicotine receptors we came across earlier. This leads to a release of dopamine and all the calming and uplifting sensations that would normally ensue if you were smoking.

This mimicking of the effect of having a smoke prevents withdrawal symptoms and therefore the craving for a real cigarette that giving up without help would provoke. You don't miss having a cigarette and giving up becomes easier.

The different forms of this therapy, which I'll come to shortly, allow you gradually to reduce the dose of nicotine you are receiving and so eventually stop the nicotine replacement therapy. You won't end up replacing one habit with another.

You still need willpower for this to work, because it doesn't compensate for all the behavioural triggers for your smoking addiction (such as enjoying a cigarette at the pub with friends, or smoking when you're stressed) but if you have this therapy prescribed on the NHS in the UK, support to stop smoking will be given alongside your NRT.

When you start on NRT, your doctor or stop-smoking advisor will suggest a dose of nicotine that roughly matches the number of cigarettes you normally smoke per day, and you will start your prescription with an agreed stop date one or even two weeks down the line.

You need to use your NRT every day and not just as and when you get your cravings, because it aims to prevent them, not just sort them out when they appear. People often find using a combination of nicotine products, such as gum with patches, allows them to fine-tune the dose of NRT more accurately to avoid cravings.

You are advised to continue treatment for two to three months to give you the best chance of long-term success.

Nicotine replacement therapies are just as bad for you as smoking.
They are actually much safer. For a start, you will not become addicted to them, because their dose is reduced over time and, second, they do not cause cancer or heart disease.

What types of NRT are available?
NRT comes in six main forms, so there should be a format to suit most people. And if one type doesn't suit you – for example, patches don't stick to your sweaty skin, or the gum gives you jaw ache – you can switch to an alternative.

Patches
These are suitable for most people, especially those who don't want to advertise the fact that they are quitting smoking, as they are hidden away under your clothes.

They come in two formats: those that you wear for twenty-four hours and those that you just wear during the daytime and take off at night (sixteen-hour patches). The twenty-four-hour patches are useful if you get really bad cravings for a cigarette as soon as you open your eyes in the morning, but the nicotine can affect some people's sleep – hence the daytime-only alternative.

Patches also come in a variety of strengths. This enables you to reduce the dose of nicotine you receive as time goes on. You will usually be prescribed (or can buy) packets of fourteen at a time and are advised to consider dropping a dose each time you get a replacement supply.

Gum

Nicotine gum comes in two strengths: 4 milligrams (for heavier twenty-plus-per-day smokers) and 2 milligrams. The nicotine is absorbed into the blood vessels in the lining of the mouth as you chew.

At first, you'll probably need to chew one piece of gum almost every hour to keep cravings at bay. The gum is chewed until the flavour becomes strongest and then you rest it in the side of your mouth until the taste fades. Then you start chewing again. The full dose will have been chewed out after around an hour.

As you get further past your quit date, you can reduce the dose of your nicotine gum by having a weaker strength, having only half a piece of gum at a time, or chewing a piece less frequently and for a shorter time.

Lozenges

Used in a very similar way to the gum, these lozenges are sucked until the flavour becomes strong and hot, and then rested in the side of the mouth until the flavour fades. You repeat this pattern until the lozenge dissolves after around half an hour.

Again, the frequency of use is reduced as time goes on.

Microtabs

These tiny tablets are designed to dissolve slowly under your tongue, without swallowing. The nicotine is absorbed into the bloodstream through the floor of your mouth and through your tongue as the tablet dissolves. You'll probably need to use one or two of these every hour or so to start with and then reduce the daily dose as you get further past your quit date.

It's advised that you continue to use microtabs for between three and six months once you've stopped smoking to prevent relapse.

Inhalators

These devices are cigarette-shaped and have been designed particularly to help people who miss the hand-to-mouth action of smoking a normal cigarette when they quit. They also work more quickly than lozenges and gum and can be used to fight cravings as soon as they start.

When you first start to quit and for the first couple of months, you will probably use the inhalator up to a dozen times a day for around twenty minutes each go. This will reduce with time. The usual length of treatment with this NRT product is twelve weeks.

Nasal spray

This method of administering a dose of nicotine is by far the fastest as the drug is absorbed very quickly into the rich blood supply inside your nose. One spray delivers the equivalent of the nicotine content of one cigarette to your brain in around ten minutes.

Again, you use the spray for about twelve weeks, starting by giving yourself one to two sprays each hour, depending on how many cigarettes you were smoking previously, and reducing the frequency towards the end of the course.

Are there any side effects?

Unfortunately, all medicines have the potential to cause side effects and some of us are more sensitive than others. In general, however, NRTs are very well tolerated, with only minor problems experienced by most users and less than 5 per cent of people reporting that they had to stop using the treatments because of their side effects.

The table opposite highlights the most common difficulties people have with the different types of NRT product.

NRT	Side effects
Patches	Skin rashes at the site of the patch (which can be helped by using creams or antihistamine tablets), poor sleep (can be prevented by switching to a sixteen-hour patch).
Gum	Bad taste, tingling tongue, hiccups, upset stomach, jaw ache.
Lozenges	Upset stomach, hiccups, flatulence, indigestion, headache.
Microtabs	Dizziness, headache, sore mouth and throat, palpitations, upset stomach, persistent runny nose (rhinitis).
Inhalator	Cough, sore throat, upset stomach.
Nasal spray	Rhinitis, watery eyes, nose bleeds, sneezing, cough, headaches, dizziness, upset stomach.

Use in pregnancy and while breastfeeding

As doctors, we try to keep pregnant women and breastfeeding mothers as drug-free as possible because of the potential risks to their babies from many prescription medicines. However, smoking presents such a high risk to the normal growth and development of babies, both before and after they're born, that if you are pregnant and can't stop smoking without help, it is recommended you try one of these NRTs. You should see your doctor or midwife for further advice.

Does NRT work?

Yes, it does work. A lot of good scientific research has been done into the effectiveness of NRT and most of the results are very positive. And when the results of these individual studies are combined and analysed, the conclusion is that using NRT increases your chances of successful quitting by a huge 50–70 per cent – which means it's got to be worth a try.

This level of success is usually achieved when people have support from a trained stop-smoking counsellor. So although you can, as I've said, buy these different NRTs over the counter from your local chemist, it's always best to get them either through your family doctor or, in the UK, from one of the NHS stop-smoking clinics that are run in libraries and community centres. Similar schemes operate in other countries, so please see Appendix B for further details about how to access them.

5

Stop-smoking drugs

If you don't want to try NRT – or are finding the side
effects too difficult to cope with – what else is available?
There are two medicines that have been licensed to help
people quit smoking. These are Champix (varenicline),
called Chantix in the USA, and Zyban (bupropion).
They work in different ways to NRT – and to each
other. Both of these medicines must be obtained on
prescription from your family doctor or stop-smoking
clinic and, in the UK, attendance at a support clinic is
mandatory before the prescription will be issued.

Champix/Chantix (varenicline)
What does it do?
The chemical shape of this drug's molecules enables
it to attach to nicotine receptors on nerve cells in

the brain. This has the effect of reducing cravings for nicotine in cigarettes, and has the same effect on withdrawal symptoms if you have stopped smoking.

Not only that, but with Champix stuck to these receptors, nicotine from cigarettes cannot attach to them if you do smoke and so you don't get any enjoyable effects from having a cigarette.

How do you take it?

In order to get the most out of this drug, you need to set yourself a quit date before you start taking it. This date should be non-negotiable and carved in stone if it is going to mean anything to you, so it needs to be sensibly thought out. For example, it should not be before a stag weekend with a bunch of smoker friends, or a wedding, or your birthday party, or any other occasion where you are likely to reach for a cigarette as part of the festivities. It could be doomed to failure almost instantaneously. Avoid times of stress too if cigarettes are your stress-buster of choice.

Once you've settled on that quit date, you then start taking the tablets one to two weeks beforehand, so the drug can build up its effectiveness. The initial doses come as a starter pack, with the dose taken increasing slowly over the first week.

So you begin with a 500 microgram tablet once daily for three days and then increase the dose to 500 micrograms twice daily for the next four days. From then on, you take a 1 milligram tablet twice daily for a further eleven weeks. This twelve-week course can be repeated, if it will help to cut down the risk of relapse.

Are there any side effects?

All medicines have potential side effects and with this one the most common are:

- stomach and bowel disturbances

- appetite changes

- a dry mouth and altered taste

- headaches

- drowsiness

- dizziness

- an upset sleep pattern

- abnormal dreams.

It is rare for people to get all of these, and rarer still for them not to settle after a few days as your body gets used to having the drug in your system.

On a more serious note, there have been rare reported cases of people becoming depressed and even suicidal while on this medicine. It's therefore advised that you let your doctor know straight away if you are taking this pill and begin to feel agitated and depressed. But this is a rare problem.

Can anyone take it?

Champix is not licensed for use by people under the age of eighteen who are trying to stop smoking. It's also not suitable for pregnant women or breastfeeding mums and, because of the depression risk mentioned above, it needs to be used with caution by people with a medical history of mental health problems.

Does it work?

It does! And researchers have found that you are three times more likely to be successful at trying to quit cigarettes using Champix than if you just go cold turkey and try to stop without help.

Zyban (bupropion)

What does it do?

This drug was initially developed as an antidepressant, but it was found that smokers being treated for depression often quitted smoking while they were on it, without really trying. It works on two neurotransmitters in the brain called dopamine and noradrenaline and raises the levels of each of them.

It's not fully understood how boosting the levels of these transmitters makes people stop smoking, but it seems to reduce cravings for cigarettes and make smoking less attractive.

How do you take it?

Zyban pills come in a dose of 150 milligrams per tablet. Like Champix, they should be started one to two weeks in advance of a planned stop date. Also like Champix, the dose starts low and builds up within the first week, so you take one tablet once per day for six days and then increase to a twice-daily dose for the rest of the course.

Most people take Zyban for between seven and nine weeks in total, but the manufacturers warn that if it hasn't worked after seven weeks, then it is unlikely to do so and might as well be stopped.

Are there any side effects?

You should always read the small print that comes with packets of pills in case you are unlucky enough to develop one of the rarer side effects a tablet can induce. With Zyban, the most commonly experienced problems are:

- a dry mouth

- gastrointestinal and taste disturbances

- agitation

- anxiety

- dizziness

- depression

- headache

- poor concentration

- insomnia

- tremor

- fever

- itching

- rash

- sweating.

Again, unless you are really unlucky, you are unlikely to be hit by all of these problems and they may wear off as your body gets used to taking the pill.

Can anyone take it?
It is not licensed for children and should be avoided during pregnancy and breastfeeding. It isn't suitable for anyone going through alcohol or benzodiazepine withdrawal, or people with cirrhosis of the liver or brain tumours. Patients with epilepsy should also avoid it, as should those who have bipolar disorder or have had anorexia or bulimia.

A reduced, once-daily, dose is recommended when the drug is taken by the elderly.

Does it work?
Success rates for Zyban are good. It has been shown to double your chances of quitting compared with a placebo treatment. It also gives a one-and-a-half times greater chance of staying off the cigarettes long term than without treatment.

6

E-cigarettes

I first became aware of e-cigarettes about five years ago on a flight from Bristol to Dublin, when the head stewardess announced over the tannoy that her colleagues would soon be passing through the cabin offering smokers the chance to purchase one of these revolutionary gadgets. They would, she informed us, allow them to have a smoke on the plane and beat the cravings they would normally have for a traditional cigarette, which they would obviously not be able to enjoy until they had collected their baggage and left the terminal building at Dublin airport.

A few hands went up, but these e-cigarettes were too far away for me to see what they looked like and what electronic smoking actually entailed. Now, of course, they are everywhere – 3 million of them were sold in the UK alone in 2012. In June 2013 the British government said they were looking to regulate them in the same way as nicotine replacement medications.

So, what are e-cigarettes, do they help smokers quit, and are they safe?

A quick bit of history

E-cigarettes were first developed in China at the turn of the millennium by a pharmacist called Hon Lik. They were designed to help smokers quit their habit and were first marketed in China for this purpose in 2004. In 2007 they received their first worldwide patents and the market for them has been expanding ever since, with 21 per cent of Americans who smoke traditional cigarettes having tried them by the end of the last decade, according to the CDC (US Centers for Disease Control). In the USA, sales of e-cigarettes doubled in 2012, raking in what's believed to be between $300 million and $500 million for their manufacturers.

What's in an e-cigarette?

These devices come in a range of shapes and sizes. Most of them are designed to look like a traditional cigarette, with a white shaft and an end that is orange and patterned like a filter tip, although there are some that are all black.

E-cigarettes have an outer casing made of plastic, so they are obviously much heavier than a traditional cigarette. They are divided into two pieces, which house the three main components of the gadget (see diagram).

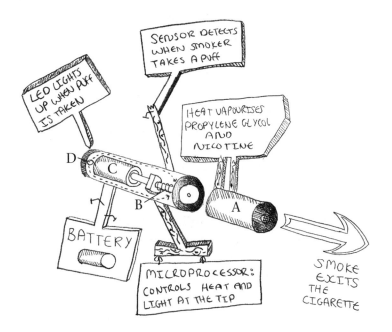

The inside of an e-cigarette

At one end there is the cartridge (A). This short barrel contains the nicotine, which comes in various strengths and is dissolved in a liquid called propylene glycol (a chemical also found in smoke machines used in stage shows). It also contains other chemicals that create different flavours in the inhaled vapours to provide users with a variety of different-tasting brands – as they would have with real cigarettes. Each cartridge contains enough liquid to produce the same number of puffs in one e-cigarette as you would get in around forty normal cigarettes. These puffs, however, contain nicotine without all the other toxins produced when tobacco is burned in traditional cigarettes.

The remainder of the device, which screws into the cartridge, contains a vaporizing chamber (B) which turns the liquid in the cartridge into a gas to be inhaled, and a rechargeable lithium battery (C) to make the whole thing work. This battery can be recharged via a USB attachment that often comes with the e-cigarette, but car and wall chargers are also available so that you can top it up at any time and almost anywhere.

Finally, there's a red LED at the very tip (D) which lights up when a user inhales and also acts as an indicator of remaining battery life by flashing repeatedly if it's about to run out.

How is it smoked?

First of all, when it comes to an e-cigarette, you need to get the terminology right: it's called "vaping" rather than smoking because there's no combustion involved and you inhale vapour rather than smoke. During vaping you place the end of the e-cigarette between your lips and breathe in, much as you would if smoking tobacco. This time, though, instead of drawing air through a filter, you do it through a small hole in the end of the device. This pulls air across a sensor in the vaporizing chamber which triggers a small coil to heat up the liquid in the cartridge and turn it into a vapour that you then inhale. At this point the red light at the tip of the e-cigarette comes on.

You then exhale excess vapour in the same way you would breathe out cigarette smoke, although, unlike with ordinary cigarettes, the vapour has no odour. All of this happens instantaneously so that it exactly imitates your usual method of smoking.

Can they help you quit?

I have a number of friends and patients who swear by these little things, and there are countless other personal testimonies all over the internet telling of how e-cigarettes have helped people stop smoking when all else has failed. I have one friend in particular who I thought would never be able to quit the habit; he even used to have a crafty cigarette when fielding at the boundary while playing cricket for our local club – no doubt looking quite the elite athlete as he did so! However, he quickly took to an e-cigarette and over the course of many months he started to puff on it less and less until eventually he quit altogether. He is now smoke-free and not only has grateful lungs but also has team mates who can rely on him to take a catch during a cricket match without having to find somewhere to stub out his cigarette first.

Unfortunately, despite the mounting anecdotal evidence of the success of these devices, very few proper research studies have so far been done to see if e-cigarettes could be recommended as stop-smoking aids for everyone. And the only one that has been published showed precious little benefit when e-cigarette quitters were compared with a group of people who quit without any help.

The other concern among the medical profession is that e-cigarettes are not yet regulated in the same way as other therapies to help people quit. As a result, there are no standard manufacturing practices and the content of nicotine and other potentially toxic ingredients in e-cigarettes ranges very widely between the companies that produce them. There's also a concern that traditional cigarette manufacturers, having seen a gap in the market and being keen to cash in, are also making e-cigarettes to try to encourage people who think these devices are safer to develop a nicotine addiction and then move on to combustible cigarettes.

The future

The British government has vowed to get e-cigarettes regulated as medicines by 2016, meaning tighter checks on safety and manufacturing standards and more research into their effectiveness as devices to help you stop smoking. Other countries are sure to do the same, meaning in future you will know exactly what's in your e-cigarette and the best way to use it to stop smoking.

In the meantime, what we do know is that the contents of e-cigarettes are a thousand times less toxic than those in traditional cigarettes, so if vaping means you get your fill of nicotine without a generous side order of toxins, it has to be a good thing. Cutting down and then stopping altogether should be your final goal though, so you need to beware of the danger of simply swapping one addiction for another.

E-cigarettes are a gateway to smoking real cigarettes.
From research that's been done so far, there's no evidence that young people are likely to try e-cigarettes and then move on to smoking tobacco.

7

Psychological support for quitting

A lot of the evidence from research into the best ways to stop smoking has pointed towards the value of having some type of psychological support while you do it. This not only provides encouragement for you to stick to your task when things get tough, but also makes you feel accountable to someone else for the progress, or lack of it, that you're making.

There is a range of ways to access this support, from face-to-face stop-smoking clinics and appointments with psychologists and therapists, to telephone counselling and smartphone apps. Here we look at what's on offer and what has and hasn't been found to help.

Stop-smoking clinics

In the UK, when NRT became available on the NHS, one condition of gaining help this way was to attend a stop-smoking clinic run by a trained stop-smoking practitioner. Appointments involve not only a discussion about and issue of prescriptions for medicines or NRT but also supportive counselling, tailored advice to help beat any cravings you might have, and encouragement to avoid relapsing.

These clinics also monitor your recovery by checking your carbon monoxide level. Watching the readings go down can be a powerful motivator to carrying on down the road to recovery and permanent abstinence.

Use of mobile phones

The United Nations has estimated that there are 6 billion people around the world with mobile phone subscriptions, with 92 per cent of adults in the UK known to own or use one. With this amount of coverage of the population, it makes sense to try to use these almost ubiquitous items as tools to help people quit smoking.

The three main approaches that are available at the moment involve using a texting service to support quitters, offering people stop-smoking apps to download from the internet, or having an actual stop-smoking advisor talk to you on the phone.

Text therapy

There is a range of services offered to smokers using text messaging to support efforts to quit (check Appendix B for details). They allow messages to be personalized to your age, sex, and ethnic group, and have the added advantage of being available whenever you are free to read them and wherever you are. This avoids the need for having to turn up for inconvenient appointments at a certain time and place, which can be off-putting and a barrier to getting the right support.

Evidence for their potential effectiveness has come from a number of research studies, the results of one of which, studying TXT2STOP, were published in the prestigious medical journal *The Lancet* in 2011.

It showed that people who signed up to this quitting support service received texts over six months, with five per day being sent to them for the first five weeks and then three texts per day for the rest of the study. Results showed that this method helped about 10 per cent of these smokers to quit. Although this is not an amazing success rate, it may be something worth trying if you find it hard to go to appointments and meetings.

Examples of texts sent in TXT2STOP study

- "To make things easier for yourself, try having some distractions ready for cravings and think up some personal strategies to help in stressful situations."

- "Why not write an action list of your reasons why you want to quit? Use it as your inspiration."

- "TXT2STOP: Think you'll put on weight when you quit? We're here to help. We'll TXT weight control and exercise tips, recipes, and motivation tips."

- "This is it! – QUIT DAY, throw away all your fags. TODAY is the start of being QUIT forever, you can do it!"

- "TXT2STOP: Quick result! Carbon monoxide has now left your body!"

- "Day4=Big day – cravings still strong? Don't worry, tomorrow will be easier! Keep your mind & hands busy. Save this txt so u can txt CRAVE to us at any time during the programme."

Mobile phone apps

With a mobile phone in almost everyone's pocket, it's not surprising that, alongside text help, if you have a smartphone you can also access quitting advice via a number of downloadable mobile phone apps that you can look at whenever it's convenient or you're finding symptoms or cravings a problem.

Some of these cost to download, whereas others, such as the one designed by the UK's National Health Service, are completely free. Apps available at the time of writing include:

- iQuit

- Stop Smoking Free

- No Smoking Life

- Coach Quit

- My Quitline

- NHS Quit Smoking.

Not all of them conform to traditional tried and tested methods for helping you quit, so if you are going to try using one, then the app from the NHS would be a good place to start.

Telephone support

If you would rather have a real person supporting you through the quitting process but would still like the flexibility of not having to attend clinics for a specified appointment because of time constraints or lack of transport, then using a telephone support line may well be a good way forward. As with the stop-smoking clinics mentioned above, telephone support will involve you speaking to qualified counsellors who can tailor the process to fit your specific needs. You will also get to know them as they follow you up, help you at tricky moments in the process, and give you accountability to someone else for going through with what you've started.

Psychological support for quitting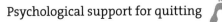

Psychotherapy

More formal talking therapies are also available to help you quit, either as a one-to-one process with a counsellor or as a group facilitated by a therapist. This type of psychological support will help you through the quitting process and to deal with some of the underlying reasons that may have got you into smoking in the first place – for example, depression, anxiety, or stress.

There are a number of different types of talking therapy around, including behavioural therapy, interpersonal therapy, cognitive behavioural therapy, and psychodynamic therapy. What they all have in common is that you will need to work in relationship with your therapist who, using the therapy in which they have expertise, can enable you to develop your own insights into how you got into smoking and the best ways for you to kick the habit. These insights will not only help tackle the factors that cause you to have psychological dependence on smoking (for example, the stress-relieving or social aspects of the habit) but also protect you from relapse in the future.

These therapies are usually available privately, but there is research evidence that suggests it would be worth the financial cost. Psychotherapy definitely increases your chance of success compared with going cold turkey.

Going cold turkey is the best way to quit any habit.

Although you do need willpower and personal commitment to give up cigarettes successfully, the evidence shows that you are much more likely to succeed if you have some sort of support from counselling or nicotine replacement therapies.

8

Alternative therapies for smoking

If you use an internet search engine to look for alternative therapies to help you stop smoking, you will be presented with around 2 million results ranging from herbs to hypnotherapy. One blogger even suggests eating dog biscuits every time you have a craving! Apparently, you'll associate the awful taste of canine treats with smoking and be desperate to quit!

Although some treatments may work for a few people, is there enough evidence for you to forgo the tried and tested prescriptions your doctor has to offer and waste your time and money on something a little less mainstream?

Here's a review of the web's top three most common suggestions. Spoiler alert! They're not that convincing!

Hypnotherapy

Hypnosis is often touted as a good treatment for a number of medical conditions such as stress, phobias, bedwetting, and impotence, as well as being effective in helping people tackle addictions. It seems, from anecdotal reports, to be really effective for some people and it's particularly appealing because, unlike prescription medicines, it doesn't have a high chance of side effects.

So what is hypnotherapy?

Hypnosis has been practised in various forms for thousands of years. It's believed to be mentioned on an ancient Egyptian papyrus from 1500 BC. But it has really taken off since the 1700s. Sigmund Freud perhaps most famously used the technique for a time to investigate the workings of the unconscious minds of his patients in nineteenth-century Vienna.

During hypnosis, hypnotherapists use a variety of techniques to bring about a trance-like state of deep relaxation. The person being hypnotized is still fully conscious (not asleep as is often thought), but, in this physically relaxed condition, their thoughts can be narrowly focused onto a particular topic while blocking out all other mental distractions.

Once hypnotized, patients are extremely open to suggestion, so the therapist is able to guide their thoughts and feelings to address a particular concern. People do need to cooperate with the process for it to work and the hypnotist cannot make them do or think things that they do not want to. This need for cooperation also explains why it doesn't work on everyone.

Research using brain scans has shown that hypnotism can change the way the brain perceives things. In one study, volunteers under hypnosis were given black-and-white objects to look at while being told by the hypnotist that these objects were coloured. On the scanner, areas of the brain that process colour lit up as they observed these objects, rather than areas that deal with black and white, as would have been expected.

What does a session involve?

Hypnotherapy sessions each last around one hour. In the first session, the therapist will begin by finding out more detail about you and your needs before explaining what will happen during your treatment.

Once you are hypnotized, probably in subsequent sessions, they will suggest ways to help you stop smoking, which may involve visualizing mental images of you achieving your goals. This will be repeated during further sessions.

This therapy is not funded by the NHS in the UK and will need to be paid for privately.

Hypnotherapy for stopping smoking

Although science has shown that hypnotherapy may have real effects on the brain, is there any evidence that it can help you quit smoking?

Some small research studies have produced promising results which suggest that it can help. I've certainly met patients who swear by it and say that they'd still be puffing away on twenty a day if it wasn't for their hypnotherapist. However, when bigger studies are done and the results of all of these are lumped together to get an overall picture, the results are not quite as convincing. It is not possible to say, hand on heart, that hypnotherapy is a reliable way to help people quit smoking and stay off the cigarettes for good.

Acupuncture

This is a form of ancient Chinese medicine, with records of its practice dating back to 200 BC. It involves inserting fine needles, made of stainless steel wire, into the skin at specific points of the body. In traditional Chinese medicine, these points are on invisible lines, or meridians, through which the body's energy, or life force, called Qi (pronounced "chee"), is believed to flow. Blocks to the flow of this energy cause illness which is then treated by acupuncture which restores the flow of Qi.

Different conditions are believed to be helped by inserting needles at different points on the body's surface and there is a range of protocols used depending upon the symptoms described by the patient and the practitioner's diagnosis.

Acupuncture for stopping smoking

In a typical consultation, it's likely that you will have a detailed history of your smoking habit taken. This will look for patterns of smoking and triggers for having a cigarette, such as after a meal or whenever you have a coffee.

Following this, the acupuncturist will carry out a physical examination. In traditional Chinese medicine, it's believed that the state of a person's tongue can help diagnose a variety of physical conditions. Therefore, as well as carrying out a physical examination in which your body will be palpated, lungs and heart listened to, and perhaps blood pressure taken, particular attention will be paid to the shape, size, colour, and coating of your tongue.

Once the assessment has been made, you will receive individually tailored treatment to meet your particular needs. This will be carried out over a number of sessions, typically five, each of which will last around one hour. During treatment, most practitioners, it seems, will concentrate on needling regions of your ear lobe, but other points on the body may also be used.

Is it effective?

Western medicine has not been successful in understanding the underlying anatomy and physiology of acupuncture points, but a fair amount of research has been done into its effectiveness as a treatment for various medical conditions. Unfortunately, there is a distinct lack of evidence for short- or long-term benefits of acupuncture when it comes to reducing withdrawal effects or helping to achieve complete cessation. In fact, when real acupuncture is compared to a sham version (which acts as a placebo), the effects are pretty similar.

It may well be a useful form of supportive treatment if you are already motivated to stop smoking, but on this evidence it certainly can't be recommended as a method for helping everyone.

Herbal treatments

St John's wort

This herbal remedy is derived from the yellow-flowered plant hypericum and has for many years been used as a treatment for depression. It's more recently been suggested as a treatment for premenstrual syndrome, ADHD, and irritable bowel syndrome, and some advocate its use to help people quit smoking.

It appears to work by affecting a number of different chemical transmitters in the brain, including serotonin, which helps boost our moods, and dopamine, which, as we've already seen, is involved in the process of becoming addicted to smoking.

Sadly, there's no evidence for it being of much real use in helping you to quit smoking. In particular, a trial in 2010, when it was compared with the effects of a placebo, those taking the sugar pills were just as likely to succeed in quitting as those on the St John's wort.

And although it's low on side effects, it is not suitable for everyone and has the added disadvantage of interacting with a number of prescription medicines. So, if you are pregnant, breastfeeding, have liver or kidney disease, are taking medicines for treating HIV, have bipolar disorder, or are taking the contraceptive pill or prescription antidepressants, it really is not for you.

Lobelia

This plant, also known as Indian tobacco, contains a chemical which acts on the brain in the same way as nicotine and causes the release of dopamine. It has therefore been touted as a natural remedy to help people stop smoking.

It does, however, have a very common side effect of nausea and vomiting, leading to its other names: pukeweed and vomitwort. And if that doesn't put you off trying it, the research into its effectiveness shows it has no benefit for quitters either.

Herbal cigarettes

Some people believe that switching to herbal cigarettes can help break the addiction to nicotine while helping you quit if part of your habit is needing something to hold and puff. They contain neither tobacco nor nicotine and are made of lovely sounding ingredients such as mint, cinnamon, rose petals, clover, cornsilk, liquorice, or lemongrass, bringing to mind the recipe for a healthy juice to drink rather than something to set fire to and smoke.

But don't be fooled by the innocuous-sounding labels on remedies that are "natural" or "herbal". They all have potential dangers. And, in the case of herbal cigarettes, the danger is that you are breathing in just as much carbon monoxide and as many potential carcinogens as you would do with a traditional cigarette.

They are therefore not recommended as a stop-smoking aid.

9

Early withdrawal symptoms

It might be a bit of a tired old cliché, but I'm afraid that the phrase "no pain, no gain" will resonate with you soon after you've stopped smoking. Addictions do not let go easily. In the first few weeks – and sometimes even months – after you've stubbed out your last cigarette, you may well experience one or two unpleasant side effects.

The good news is that you'll also gain some far more important health benefits during this period too, and we'll come to them in the next chapter. But for now let's get the bad news out of the way. Here's a rundown of some of the hardships that you will have to endure if you're going to give up smoking for good.

Cough

Ironically, your smoker's cough may be replaced by an ex-smoker's cough for a good few weeks after you've stopped. This is triggered by the recovery of some of the protective mechanisms in your lungs which had been paralysed while you were smoking.

In particular, there is a rapid recovery of the cilia, the minute hairs that line your bronchial tubes and which normally beat in unison to push germ-infested mucus away from the depths of your lungs so that it can be swallowed, spat out, or coughed up.

Smoking harms these little hairs so that the mucus, with trapped bacteria stuck to it, sinks down into the lungs instead, which explains why smokers tend to pick up chest infections more easily than non-smokers. As the cilia recover, this mucus conveyor belt springs back into action again and it starts to shift out of your lungs all the tar, toxins, and stale old mucus that has built up while you've been smoking. This stuff will irritate and trigger a cough to try to help you clear it completely.

This cough may be helped by drinking plenty of fluids such as water and fruit juice. If it doesn't settle or gets progressively worse, you ought to be checked out by your doctor.

Cold and flu-like symptoms

Alongside the cough, you may also get a constellation of other upper respiratory symptoms sometimes referred to as quitter's flu. These symptoms will include a runny nose, a sore throat, and congested sinuses, and are another result of your airways and mucous membranes coming back to life again.

This "flu" will start soon after quitting but clear within a few weeks. Hot drinks can help clear the sinuses, but in general there's no magic available to settle the symptoms and you just have to weather the storm.

Headaches

You will invariably be at risk of having more headaches than usual during the early days of your new smoke-free life and they will often coincide with the respiratory symptoms we've just looked at and so form part of the symptom package of quitter's flu.

A number of factors seem to be responsible for these headaches, including:

- nicotine withdrawal – thought to cause pain due to triggering vasodilation of blood vessels around the brain

- changes in the levels of a neurotransmitter called serotonin, which occur during addiction recovery

- tiredness because of withdrawal-related insomnia (see below).

Simple over-the-counter painkillers such as paracetamol (acetaminophen) and ibuprofen should be enough to give you some relief. The headaches will be less severe if you can make sure you have adequate rest and stay well hydrated in those first few weeks after quitting.

Insomnia

Although some quitters feel tired all the time in the first few weeks after stopping (because their brains are missing the stimulant effects of nicotine), many more will suffer from insomnia and find getting any decent sleep a real problem. The most likely reason for this is a difference in the way that caffeine (a stimulant found in tea, coffee, and energy drinks and known to affect sleep) is metabolized in smokers and non-smokers.

Nicotine speeds up the metabolism of caffeine so that when smokers have a tea or coffee, they only get around half the dose of caffeine that a non-smoker does. When they stop smoking, the dose they get is effectively doubled, resulting in an increase in its stimulant effects and a decrease in sleep.

To get around this, the obvious suggestion is to cut down on drinks containing caffeine and maybe swap them for decaffeinated alternatives or herbal tea. A cup of warm milk before bed can really help too.

Weight gain

This one is the biggie: the side effect that seems to put most people off and make them throw in the towel. Smokers might be worried about the condition of their heart and lungs and their risk of developing a terminal illness, but this concern pales into insignificance for some when confronted with the possibility that if they quit smoking they will get fat!

Research has shown that on average, one year after stopping smoking, quitters put on 4–5 kilograms in weight, with 13 per cent putting on up to 10 kilograms. However, 16 per cent will lose weight over this time.

Nicotine is an appetite suppressant, so, as long as people smoke, their habit encourages them to eat less. Once the nicotine is gone, the appetite returns and with it comes the weight gain. It can be entirely avoided if you fill up on fruit and avoid sugary and fatty snacks.

And, if not, it's surely a small price to pay.

As the Roy Castle FagEnds website puts it, would you rather be:

(a) a slightly overweight non-smoker or

(b) underweight and dead?

They've got a point!

Constipation
Because nicotine has an effect on the digestive system, you may notice that your guts start to misbehave as you wean yourself off it and they try to get themselves back to normal. The most frequent complication is that you will open your bowels less frequently and may feel quite bunged up.

This tends to be an early side effect which settles by the end of the first month. To try to avoid it, make sure you eat fruit and vegetables until they're coming out of your ears, have bran and roughage for breakfast, and wash it all down with plenty of water and fruit juice.

Mood changes and irritability

Given that you'll feel fluey, have thumping headaches, be getting little sleep, have bunged-up bowels, and be putting on weight, it perhaps won't come as a surprise that you may well feel a bit grumpy and irritable after you've quit smoking.

But irritability, low mood, and anxiety can also be direct effects of the nicotine-withdrawal process itself and not just a consequence of being dragged down emotionally by all the other unpleasant side effects of stopping smoking. And it's also believed that part of the depression that can occur at this time is due to mourning the loss of the things that you associate with smoking – the camaraderie with other smokers and the social side of the habit.

This feeling of being bereaved can last a couple of months, but it can be helped by finding other positive ways to spend your time and by keeping busy, rather than simply hanging out in old haunts which remind you of what you've lost.

It will be worth it!

This list of possible "quitting" symptoms might make you not want to bother at all. I'll be honest: they're certainly not that appealing.

But it must be remembered that, first, they may not happen to you at all (and certainly nicotine replacement and other medical treatments for withdrawal can help keep them at bay) and, second, if you do experience these symptoms, they will all be short-lived.

In contrast, the consequences of keeping up your habit will be far more significant and the only thing that may be short-lived is you!

So, on a more positive note, the next chapter looks at the beneficial changes that happen to your body as you recover from the effects of smoking. And, thankfully, they far outweigh the negatives we've just looked at. By a mile!

 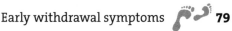

10

Health benefits of quitting

Because smoking has such a wide-ranging effect on pretty much all of your body, here's a head-to-toe rundown of what you can look forward to if you kick the habit.

Face
Vain creatures that we are, most of us spend a lot of time and money on grooming and trying to look good. In fact, a report in 2013 by a Harley Street beauty clinic suggested that women spend 474 days of their lives sitting in front of a mirror putting on make-up. Other surveys have found that men spend even more time than that on washing, shaving, and moisturizing.

Stop smoking and your skin texture will look better all by itself, without the need for expensive creams and lotions – surely a big point in its favour. This is because the skin of non-smokers gets a better supply of oxygen and nutrients. By stopping, you can reverse the wrinkly complexion that appears more rapidly due to cigarette damage.

Your teeth will also be healthier and whiter if you stop smoking, and you will be less prone to gum disease. And, of course, your breath will smell fresher.

Senses

Your sense of both taste and smell will come back to life again, having been dulled by the toxic effects of the chemicals in your cigarettes. You'll be able to enjoy food more and experience the wonderful smell of freshly cut grass once again.

Lung capacity

You will breathe much more easily and cough much less if you give up smoking. Lung capacity improves by around 10 per cent in the first year after quitting, allowing you to exercise more effectively, or simply to get up the stairs without being severely out of puff and needing a sit down when you get to the top.

Circulation

Circulation improves even more quickly than your breathing, often within the first month of quitting.

This will give you more energy for physical activity, and warmer hands and feet.

Immunity
Quitting will give a boost to your immune system and so, when firing on all cylinders, it will offer much better protection against colds and flu and all the chest infections you will have picked up as a smoker.

Sex
With better teeth and skin, you're much more likely to be attractive to a prospective partner if you give up smoking – and your kisses will no doubt taste sweeter too. Perhaps more importantly, when men stop smoking they get better erections, and, with improved circulation to those sensitive areas and erogenous zones, sex can become more intense and result in heightened orgasms for men and women.

Fertility also improves, with men producing healthier sperm and miscarriage becoming less likely after a successful conception.

So it's definitely a win-win situation in the bedroom if you stop smoking.

Emotions
Research has shown that, after quitting, your stress levels decrease and you will be less angry and irritable than if you continued smoking. There also seems to be an inverse relationship between the amount you smoke

and the levels of a brain chemical called serotonin. So the more you smoke, the less serotonin you have, and the less serotonin you have, the more likely you are to feel depressed and contemplate suicide.

If you stop smoking, your serotonin levels will go back to normal and your sense of mental well-being will quickly improve.

Life expectancy

The icing on the benefits-of-stopping-smoking cake has got to be that you will live longer. This is an indisputable fact. Smoking, as we've already seen, lays you open to developing all kinds of lethal diseases that will happily kill you off before your natural expiry date. Cancer, heart disease, and strokes all have a wealth of experience of curtailing people's lives well before they're ready to go. And they are more likely to get you if you smoke.

But if you stop smoking at the age of thirty, you'll get ten more years than you would have had as a smoker. Even if you leave it as late as sixty to pack in the habit, you still gain at least an extra three years that you would have otherwise missed out on.

A new you!

With all of these benefits coming your way, you'd surely be crazy not to have a go at quitting. You'll look and feel better, the air will smell sweeter, you'll be "hotter" between the sheets, and you'll be around longer to enjoy it all!

Length of time	Health benefits
20 minutes	Your heart rate goes back to normal.
2 hours	Your blood pressure goes back to normal. Withdrawal symptoms start, such as cravings, anxiety, and frustration.
12 hours	Blood levels of toxic carbon monoxide reduce to normal and there's a corresponding increase in your blood oxygen.
24 hours	Your risk of having a heart attack has already started to drop.
3 days	Nicotine has now left your body and the withdrawal symptoms will be at their peak.
2–3 weeks	Improvements in your lung function and circulation will mean you begin to feel better and are able to be more active without feeling you're going to peg out.
9 months	Lung function is back to normal. You'll breathe more easily, cough less, and be at less risk of chest infections.
1 year	Your risk of heart disease has dropped by 50 per cent.
5 years	Your risk of having a stroke is now the same as for a person who has never smoked.
10 years	Your risk of developing cancer of the lungs, mouth, throat, oesophagus, kidney, bladder, and pancreas is now 50 per cent lower than it was when you smoked.
15 years	Your risk of developing heart disease will now be the same as that of a non-smoker.

Mythbuster

I've smoked for so long now that the damage is done.

The damage done by smoking is cumulative; whenever you stop, you will reap the health benefits of not continuing.

A final word

I hope that the evidence I've provided in this book has left you in no doubt that smoking is bad news. It may kill you if you continue with it, and its choice of murder weapons is extensive: cancer of pretty much any organ you care to name, heart attacks, strokes, and the long, slow, lingering death of a chronically suffocating lung disease.

But it needn't be that way. It's never too late to stop and there have never been more effective ways to help you try than are available now. You will need willpower and it may not be an easy ride, with many false starts and failures along the way. But it will be one of the best things you ever do. It will extend your life, improve its quality, and give you more time to spend with those you love.

Unfortunately, no one can do it for you, and if you don't want to, then all the warnings in the world won't do any good. But if you're convinced the time is right, don't waste any more time or money – just go for it. You owe it to yourself and your family to give it your best shot.

If that's you, then Appendix B has lists of how to access all the resources you'll need to get you started. And I wish you all the best as you take your first steps towards a smoke-free future!

Appendix A: Anatomy of a cigarette

The main components of a cigarette

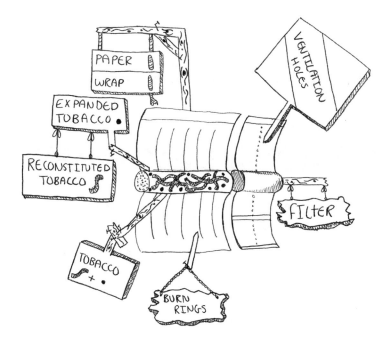

PAPER WRAP

EXPANDED TOBACCO

RECONSTITUTED TOBACCO

VENTILATION HOLES

FILTER

TOBACCO + .

BURN RINGS

What's inside?

Unlike the food you buy from a supermarket, you don't get a list of ingredients on the side of a pack of cigarettes to let you know exactly what you are breathing in. Instead, if you can be bothered, you have to go looking on the manufacturers' websites to find out in any detail what they contain, and even then they only tell you the innocuous-sounding functions these ingredients perform in the cigarette – for example, adding flavour, forming part of the filter, or adhesive to stick the outer paper down.

But that's far from the whole story where many of the ingredients are concerned. So here's a list of some of the chemicals contained in all cigarettes, alongside their more toxic uses. If you're squeamish, you might want to look away now!

Ingredient	What's bad about it?
Ammonia	Used as a household cleaner
Angelica root extract	Known to cause cancer in animals
Arsenic	Used in rat poisons
Benzene	Used in making dyes, synthetic rubber
Butane	Gas, used in lighter fluid
Cadmium	Used in batteries
Carbon monoxide	Poisonous gas
Cyanide	Deadly poison
DDT	A banned insecticide

Ethyl furoate	Causes liver damage in animals
Formaldehyde	Used to preserve dead specimens
Lead	Poisonous in high doses
Methoprene	Insecticide
Methyl isocyanate	Its accidental release killed 2,000 people in Bhopal, India, in 1984
Napthalene	Ingredient in mothballs
Polonium	Cancer-causing radioactive element

This list goes a long way to explaining why all packets have to carry a health warning and why cigarettes are often known as cancer sticks. And I'm afraid it doesn't matter what type of cigarette you smoke – be it high- or low-tar, all cigarettes are made the same. So don't be fooled into thinking that you are doing yourself a favour by switching to low-tar brands; there are just as many heavy duty toxins in "lights".

Some unlucky numbers

Here's an idea of the true scale of the toxic nature of cigarettes. Each one contains:

• 4,000 chemicals of which
• 40 are known to be cancer-causing and
• 400 are known to be toxic in other ways.

Appendix B:
Useful information

There are a number of both government-funded and charity-run organizations around the world aimed at helping you to quit smoking. Their websites are not only a mine of information but also contain links that allow you to access telephone helplines, text messaging services, and one-to-one support.

The list below is far from exhaustive but provides useful starting points to help set you off in the right direction for a new smoke-free life.

United Kingdom
ASH (Action on Smoking and Health)
ASH is a campaigning public health charity, set up in 1971, with the aim of working towards eliminating the harm caused by tobacco. It not only campaigns at a government level for policies to reduce the dangers of tobacco but also advises smokers about ways to stop.

6th floor, Suites 59–63
New House
67–68 Hatton Garden
London EC1N 8JY
Telephone: 0207 404 0242
Website: www.ash.org.uk

QUIT

This charity aims to help smokers stop and to prevent
young people from starting smoking. Their services
include helplines and community programmes in eight
different languages.

20–22 Curtain Road
London EC2A 3NF
Telephone: 0207 539 1700
Website: www.quit.org.uk

Roy Castle Lung Cancer Foundation

A charity named after British entertainer Roy Castle,
a non-smoker who died of lung cancer in 1994. It
supports research into lung cancer and provides advice
about how to stop smoking.

The Roy Castle Centre
4–6 Enterprise Way
Wavertree Technology Park
Liverpool L13 1FB
Telephone: 0333 323 7200
Website: www.roycastle.org

Smokefree
This is the NHS stop-smoking resource centre. It includes web and telephone advice and will point you in the direction of your nearest local stop-smoking clinics and groups.

Telephone: 0800 022 4 332
Website: http://smokefree.nhs.uk

Australia
Each state has its own stop-smoking helplines but the following are run nationally.

Smokenders
An organization run by ex-smokers which helps people quit by addressing the physical, social, psychological, and emotional aspects of smoking addiction and without the use of medication.

Telephone: 1800 021 000
Website: www.smokenders.com.au

Quitline
This is the official government website giving advice about all aspects of smoking and ways to quit, as well as offering support.

National Tobacco Campaign
Social Marketing & Partnerships
Australian National Preventive Health Agency

GPO Box 462
Canberra City ACT 2601
Telephone: 13 7848
Website: www.quitnow.gov.au

Canada

Healthy Canadians

This is the official government site, which includes advice about quitting, details of sources of help, and a calculator to allow you to see how many dollars you could save by giving up.

Health Canada
Address Locator 0900C2
Ottawa, Ontario
K1A 0K9
Telephone: 1 866 225 0709
Website: http://healthycanadians.gc.ca/health-sante/tobacco-tabac/index-eng.php

Smokers' Helpline

Offers free one-to-one telephone help, text message support, and an online quit programme.

Telephone: 1 877 513 5333
Website: www.smokershelpline.ca

New Zealand

Quitline

A charity-run service funded by the Ministry of Health aimed at helping all New Zealanders quit smoking. It has a particular interest in working with Maori people and pregnant women. Offers advice about quitting treatments and one-to-one support.

Quitline
PO Box 12 605
Wellington
Telephone: 0800 778 778
Website: www.quit.org.nz

United States of America

Smokefree.gov

This countrywide resource is provided by the National Cancer Institute. It offers a step-by-step stop-smoking guide and advice about where to access more detailed help in every state. It also provides a text messaging service and a telephone quit line.

Telephone: 1 877 44U QUIT (1 877 448 7848)
Website: www.smokefree.gov